Staged

Imerald Brown

Copyright © 2021 Imerald Brown

All rights reserved.

ISBN: 9798567663011

DEDICATION

To Vera Mae Walton, Levi Brown, Alma Louise Nevels, Charles Stalling, J.B. Brown, and Linda Nevels. I have experienced profound loss like many people. Death has been a lesson. My mother, Linda Nevels, prepared me when I was young. My mother's intentions weren't intended to harm me emotionally. Yet, her insights on death were crushing to my young heart.

As an adult, I now understand that she was teaching me the reality that life cannot exist without death. When my mother passed away, she had a soothing smile on her face. She wasn't afraid. She embraced her transition bravely. I can only imagine the fearlessness she inhibited while leaving this world.

This book is for my loved ones that I have lost over the years. My daily life is filled with reflection, acceptance and even denial at times. I go through the stages of grief. I cry. I remember. I laugh. Loosing immediate family members has been a never-ending teaching moment. I have come to look at life from a fresh perspective. Not just one perspective. Perspectives shift and morph. They are not absolute.

What you will read here is an opened mind. My opened mind. A mind that's traveling in the ethers of Universe. I did not write this book, some Thing beyond me did. I am just a messenger utilized in mind.

CONTENTS

Acknowledgments	i
Act 1	Pg #3
Act 2	Pg #4
Act 3	Pg #5
Act 4	Pg #6
Act 5	Pg #7
Act 6	Pg #9
Act 7	Pg #11
Act 8	Pg #12
Act 9	Pg #15
Act 10	Pg #17
Act 11	Pg #19
Act 12	Pg #21
Act 13	Pg #23
Act 14	Pg #25
Act 15	Pg #27
Act 16	Pg #29
Act 17	Pg #31

STAGED

Act 18	Pg #33
Act 19	Pg #35
Act 20	Pg #36
Act 21	Pg #39
Act 22	Pg #41
Act 23	Pg #42
Act 24	Pg #43
Act 25	Pg #45
Act 26	Pg #47
Act 27	Pg #50
Act 28	Pg #52
Act 29	Pg #54
Act 30	Pg #55
Act 31	Pg #56
Act 32	Pg #57
Act 33	Pg #59
Act 34	Pg #60
Act 35	Pg #62
Act 36	Pg #63
Act 37	Pg #64

STAGED

Act 38	Pg #65
Act 39	Pg #66
Act 40	Pg #67
Act 41	Pg #68
Act 42	Pg #69
Act 43	Pg #70
Act 44	Pg #71
Act 45	Pg #72
Act 46	Pg #74
Act 47	Pg #76
Act 48	Pg #77
Act 49	Pg #78
Act 50	Pg #80
Act 51	Pg #82
Act 52	Pg #83
Act 53	Pg #84
Act 54	Pg #86
Act 55	Pg #88
Act 56	Pg #90
Act 57	Pg #92

STAGED

Act 58	Pg #95
Act 59	Pg #97
Act 60	Pg #99
Act 61	Pg #101
Act 62	Pg #103
Act 63	Pg #105
Act 64	Pg #106
Act 65	Pg #108
Act 66	Pg #109
Act 67	Pg #111
Act 68	Pg #112
Act 69	Pg #113
Act 70	Pg #115
Act 71	Pg #117
Act 72	Pg #119
Act 73	Pg #120
Act 74	Pg #121
Act 75	Pg #123
Act 76	Pg #125
Act 77	Pg #127

STAGED

Act 78	Pg #129
Act 79	Pg #131
Act 80	Pg #133
Act 81	Pg #134
Act 82	Pg #136
Act 83	Pg #138
Act 84	Pg #139
Act 85	Pg #140
Act 86	Pg #141
Act 87	Pg #142
Act 88	Pg #143
Act 89	Pg #145
Act 90	Pg #146
Act 91	Pg #147
Act 92	Pg #149
Act 93	Pg #150
Act 94	Pg #152
Act 95	Pg #154
Act 96	Pg #156
Act 97	Pg #159

STAGED

Act 98	Pg #161
Act 99	Pg #163
Act 100	Pg #165
Act 101	Pg #167
Act 102	Pg #169
Act 103	Pg #170
Act 104	Pg #172
Act 105	Pg #173
Act 106	Pg #174
Act 107	Pg #175
Act 108	Pg #177
Act 109	Pg #179
Act 110	Pg #181
Act 111	Pg #183
Act 112	Pg #185
Act 113	Pg #187
Act 114	Pg #189
About the Author	Pg #190

ACKNOWLEDGMENTS

I want to send my older brother love. Big brother you have made a tremendous impact on my creativity. You have been through so many storms and I just want you to know that I love you. To my sister, I love you and I am so happy for the life you have created for yourself.

To Señor Gigio, the illustrator of Staged; I am so grateful for your creations, I see your light.

ACT 1

I am befriending my psyche
infiltrate and gather

I stand with my mission and agenda

Patterns play theatrical
the sky is my stage light

ACT 2

Bound by the absence and nothingness
    inspiration has no substantive restraints

Worldly laws have no grasp on my scribbles
    unconfined streams

Comfortably dodging borders
    placed there to hinder connection - of what has always been

Belly flopping in endless supply
    a diet would be foreign

Feast and fill up
    Give because there is more where it came from

ACT 3

I am as empty as a giver
These thoughts know nothing
    they are unreliable

This voice speaks
    but utterances undefined

My body moves unlike my mind
I am losing my container of spirit
Noticing the unfamiliar
    insanely detached

ACT 4

I have complained
    came down with a world filled with calamity

My control room malfunctioned
    attempting to solve matters I am divorced from

But these hands pry and these eyes snoop
In parallel, the world I hold keys for
    maintained the floods
    and welcomed more of the outpour

I ignored my wheel and anxiously gripped yours
    Sweet distraction

A view of something more dramatic

I am comfort's keeper
    allowing myself to become wrapped in them

My messes have not been cleansed of debris
The attention pays
    and the morning's residue
    remain throughout the day

My mirror covered in cloth and forgotten

"I would not dare do such things"
    my ego boastfully cheers

There is no challenge, I react in default
    a sprinter - running away from my ownerships

ACT 5

I wish for typos and missed spelled words to kome
    I wish for the absence of hunger

I wish for fullness in our bellies
    and fullness in our subconsciousness

I wish the fullness leaves us empty
I wish we can say "no, but thanks"
    and be okay with what we have got

This littleness is disguised
This littleness is a cover up
    what's behind is Grand

I feel it beyond this body - this body is not mine
This body is temporary
    I just use it in the meantime

I crave mistakes and forgiveness
I crave the forgiveness of self
I wish for typos and missed spelled words to kome

Trends of transparency
Trends of perfection
    when does intentional become automatic?

Empty of thoughts and defining symbols
No thing to protect
I carry no weight
Moments of surrender
Moments of clarity

STAGED

A glimpse of peaceful fear
This fear is heavy on my heart

In the void of detachment with nothing to anchor me
I float in Love and fear hides
        because fear is terrified of Love

STAGED

ACT 6

You contain essence profoundly unspeakable
To utter your magic descriptively
    would be a disservice

Mechanical and fixed with codes
Containment of love and soul

I am in debt

My confession is
    I foolishly misused you in many ways

Guilt misuses you more
How can I know this yet continue to place
    such harsh circumstances upon you?

The responsibility is an undertaking noble
To rejoice in what causes ill manufactures disasters

The fires have engulfed you
    and you have become inflamed

Foolishly in my Knowing
    I chose to look the opposite way

I violently let you burn
    all while a well inches away

Torturously sabotaging
    the one thing I've known that enabled
    and made thoughts real

STAGED

Unappreciative of how you brought life through
Reflected the beauty of a simple pebble
The beauty of a gentle breeze
The beauty of startling sound pulsing through We
It is a privilege to experience these
    moments of illusion

A privilege, I have forgotten
I forgot because of the distractions
    and noise souped with clutter

The dark was always the light
Lesson neither wrong nor right
But I'm starting to love you with no binds

I've begun to realize that the privilege is limited
    and sadly - bound in this life's time

Will you sigh in relief
    when I empty the well on our lingering blaze?

I seek forgiveness because what I perceive was
    a war so vicious

Yet, knowing you as I believe I do
Wouldn't forgive but embrace the outpour of Love -
from the well inches away

If I save you
I'm saving us
My apology is self-centered and forced
I'm sorry for the flames
Thank God for this body - Thank God for this well

ACT 7

At times I am embarrassed to be human
I am ashamed of my animalistic ways

Did you create me this way?

Or is this battle a part of your puzzling, majestic game?

I am saddened and riddled with filth
I must be cleansed from the inside out
I have been wicked while walking
    these wet alleyways past midnight

The gloom fills me with every breath
But some do not feel ashamed - unlike me
Many times, I wish I could be lodged
    in their comfort and content

Carrying on in the absence of care
I feel my heart squeezed
    stabbing pain

I would like to be released
Soaked and shivering
    my eyes sing tears of mourn

I curl timidly at the sound of your scold
I hear you everywhere

ACT 8

All this growing up and changes
I haven't really noticed the changin'
I just happened automatically
        I woke up and here I was

A character - gliding through storylines
        written by my unconscious

Led by the fabrics woven by a thought system
        developed by multiple sources

A magnet of information
Dumped on like an island of piled waste
        but I am no victim of chance or stagnancy

I leave one dream in favor of another
Challenging the systems
        that struggle to remain latched

I attack self at the expense of ridding
        the sour and spoiled former

I pluck away the hairy mold
        and sponge away at the rotten

In new moments - an opportunity of birth
I choose life because living death has no taste

A bland and terrible palette
I would rather smell the full aromas
Taste the bitter in combination of the sweet

STAGED

Igniting my senses in a burst of rainbow
    with colors I haven't seen

I feel more intensely
Empathetic and unashamed
I extend my love and grace
No expectation for you to do the same

I don't expect
    but I sincerely wish

In the white parts of the pages
in-between the spaces
There exists a gap
Within that space
    love was never written

Could It be found outside that gap?

This character wishes that
love would come outside from its hiding place
    and touch lives identical to mine and unalike

I need love to fuel and renew
To be at one with my creator
To heal through my stages of character development
Love must be embedded
As the foundation
    in my contemporary thought system

A building block of humanity
We grow alone and together
Our growth benefits one and then another
Love and growth are one

STAGED

I love myself so much I choose to grow
I love you so much I choose to become better for us

I choose life
My life involves us
With love and hope
I pray
        for love's scribbles in-between the gaps

ACT 9

Covered scars
The stigma - cold hearted

You push away farther
creating empty spaces
Compulsion and paranoia
   is at the front door

Please put the blade away

Consumed
   taken over by mind itself

The shadow craves visibility
   alone and no one understands

You are treasured
   even when outcasted

STAGED

Renewed

Lingering

Bathing in Awe

Act 10

All along I did not know
It was a secret kept
For if I had the knowledge
I would not know Thirst
I am one of the lucky ones
Some never glimpse
Some transcend carrying the Thirst

Here I am
In-between
At times - a roaring anger

Magnetic pulse
Fending off the lies
Scrubbing away at filth

I have been used
Over and over
Journey of kiln born clay teacups

STAGED

Act 11

I feel nothing
    not even the beauty of a rose in a dry desert

My mirror is vacant - vacant as I stand there
My plea is for
    a heart to be reborn

Mine

Make a recipe with ingredients full of love
My plea - recreate the centerpiece

Mine

Once upon a dusk time
I was broken and lost

Mine

Between innocence
    and a life I will never know

Give me

Mine

So, I can feel pain again
    and hope

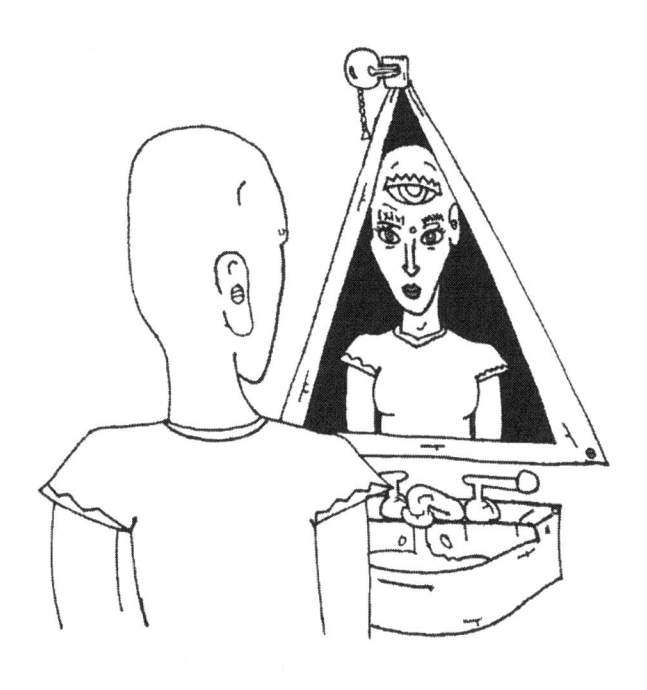

STAGED

STAGED

Act 12

adjustments
fluid
flow
morphed
mirrors
images
consumed in dialogue
teaching and receiving

Jewels Sacred

i learn in similarities and oddities
as I judge the differences
burying my anchor below Earth's crust
firm and unshaken in Self

reaching out tentacles and tapping my antenna
although, my truth is different
i hold room in many spaces
allowing the white noise of grey

hearing when it's uncomfortable to stay
hope feels heavy enough to carry
submerged in lite light
although, the Truth is we are One

i struggle against the beliefs held
the judgement simmers - fogging up the mirror
i strive to see beyond the blur

STAGED

release pressure
sighs of comfort
i am and they are
we exist because of love
we dwell in spaciousness
i intend to dismantle the illusion
seeing only Purity
smudges must be removed

STAGED

Act 13

The pathway is laid out for you
Do you dare to enter?
For entering will brew a tonic remarkable
    only the bravest are welcomed

Have you proven yourself?
Have you withstood the swaying wind amidst
    the soles of your callus feet?

Did you do the unbearable? Or rise when brutality struck?

Have you wept as much as the clouds?

Did those tears bring life to seeds of thought
    or did those tears break you in pieces a part?

There is a hum from the beginning
    do you resonate with the ALL ONE?

For if you do the breeze of this air should be
    as swift as the mountains you tend to push

Feathers of destinations
A remembering of the forces
You would have jumped
If only you'd had known you had vigorous wings
    and wind to guide you

STAGED

A call onto you
A silent shout
In hopes you'd believe in the unseen
Vibrationally loud

The hum holds us together
The music is our lives
Are you in tuned with the rhythm and cycles of beat?
I'd wish you'd hum
Hum loud enough for me

Act 14

Refraining from self and temptation
Allowing the highest good to emerge
Discipline peaks through tiny crevices
My will at times disappears like spirits' silhouettes
I am contemplating
    and back peddling to my very first step

A perception seen too many times
I could walk with eyes closed
Patterns created threads of entanglement
Trapped in panic rooms - a result of my own

These thoughts are homegrown
Something I am used to
A safe place
Infinite mirrors of doom

Addicted to the notion of suffering
I'm guilty of harm
I haven't conquered
    something this almighty before

Decades of war
Solely - in my own battlefield
A mess I fabricated
If I keep my eyes here
Forever this will be
If I close my eyes - it would be a struggle to unsee
Still, I win - in defeat

STAGED

Act 15

bland
dull
excitement
tasteless
entertainment
spectrums
categories
names
labels and brands
chasing
out of breath can barely stand
observing the normal of what i call chaos
intertwined and weaved in my projector
paragraphs and run on sentences
too fatigued to comprehend
rinsed and squeezed
drained and dry
most times i
don't practice what i'm preaching
i'm just as ignorant as a toddler
watching this world while making innocent mistakes
i question
my curiosity binges
digging deep
as deep as caverns
and the more I know
the more I have not learned
the more I tread the more it seems to hurt
minimal changes
cycles packaged creatively
disguised as something modern

STAGED

alone in the womb - identical in present day
the watcher of drama and writer of plays
identification no not of flesh
but something limitless
expedition through this time and place
i have gathered
unforgettable lessons
art against my eyelids
i ponder
if the colors are smothered
on the palms of my hands
surprised i ask
"am I the Source of it all?"
a statue in motion
at times i forget
hollowness is the means for my enlightenment
a need for wanting distorts
I release and create a spare dream

Act 16

I love superficially

Does that bother you?

I love deep as a resonating sound
    that vibrates to the core of everything

Does that bother you too?

I am in awe of how you appear before me
    and stunned by your inner display

Your insights tangle my mind
    into a web of intrusion

I want more of your intelligence

Does that frighten you?

Are you willing to be an aged, opened book?

I haven't turned pages in a while - and I miss reading

Your sustenance is ravishing
I'm sure I wouldn't be lukewarm
Right now, you are my only distraction

I have hopes
I'm sure I'll be disappointed

Nowadays no one's as transparent as they claim

STAGED

What you display is only what you'd like for me to see
I know there's something more beneath
I'll take what I can get
You may not be ready to unleash
What you don't even know intellectually
    but feel emotionally

If we continue this - and love emerges
Maybe I'll be your savior
Maybe I'll flee
Love saved - love made me leave

Act 17

She danced effortlessly
Every move filled with natural ease
Connection instantaneously
    but we were young and full of dreams

It was a time of innocence
A time of discovery
A bind never forgotten
The urgency of our company
    made time never enough

Forever wasn't a dream
Something we childishly believed
    we were content with that

I learned love
Thanks for the lesson

You learned love
I regret being an inadequate teacher

We learned profound pain
The kind that feels like a slow death

The kind that feels like
    we failed to swallow and choked

We taught each other
That love doesn't always feel good
    but in fact - unspeakably hurts

STAGED

I can't recall who provoked those feelings first

What I did was a tragedy
A calamity of fragmented hearts

I had all I wanted and needed
Still - that wasn't enough

Act 18

Love me beside the Almond Trees
Let's dare to cast away our troubles
Our foundation has been tilted
Let's be like those branches and reach new heights

Our souls are starving for us to win in this mission
We amuse them with our antics
    and our petty plays

Love me beside the Almond Trees
Where it's quiet and only our souls speak
We've done enough digging and analysis
They want to guide
    we should let them

We've been caught up in our ways
Too stubborn and stupid to change

Love me beside the Almond Trees
Let the rain deep cleanse our bodies
    washing away our grime

They want us to flow and absorb each other
Just like the nourishing water in the soil
    that keeps those Almond Trees fruitful

Our souls want us to bear fruit
    and offer each other nourishment

STAGED

We've starved one another

I want to grow so I can give you Almonds
    just like those trees do

I want to be bountiful

So, love me beside the Almond Trees
Don't love me purposely
Love me with ease

Listen to our souls
Listen to our hearts as they sync
I'm waiting for you to take me
    when you're ready - back to the Almond Trees

Act 19

Burying pain
    in hopes it will never be found again

Evil showed up unexpectedly - cries for help
    yet no one cared to listen

The secrets kept quiet - behind walls
    nobody knew

Act 20

I'd like to go
I'd say I'll go
That day comes
    and I'm distant in a faraway land

In solitude - I wouldn't want you to see me as I am
I've given up on pretending
I'm sorry I was a no show at the party
My mind wanted to go
    just blame my inflamed body

I have plenty of secrets
I am crying inside
You'd never tell
I look perfectly fine
    but this fatigue grips me and I feel drunk

I'm swaying as I walk - but I am not drunk
Your party indeed, I'd like to come
I'd see happy faces - hear laughter as it becomes one
    synchronized joy filling the room

My eyes dilated
You could probably see clearly into my haze
I'm frightened when my heart palpitates

I look fine
But
I'm
Unwell inside

STAGED

I try to show compassion
At times, I resent my flesh
I've become so selfish
I disappeared below the moon
Howled in bitterness
Years that belonged to me - burglarized
Gone but not quite forgotten

My pity longs for a new reality
My pity longs for understanding
My pity is a product of suffering

Alone and confused

How many times must my eyes swell with tears?
How can I be so fearless and still conquered by fear?
I've fallen to the floor in prayer and surrender
    I've closed my heart

I've felt defeated - I've been fighting for life
    and the fog makes it seem like I've lost my dear mind

I was afraid you'd ask, "what's wrong?"
Or "how come you're always exhausted?"
The story is too long to tell
    I feel dizzy as a pigeon flying in circles

Trembling at no threat
I tremble just because
Gasp for air like there was nothing there
My weakened leg and heavy arm

Unpredictably, I fall numb
Unpredictable I am - not because I want to
Fatigued - no amount of caffeine can undertake
I wait
I wait until my flare subsides
I feel okay at times
Unpredictable
My storm swarms in and the wind sends me tumbling
My kind of party...
I'm sorry I couldn't make it to yours
    It's a lot better there than here, I'm sure

Act 21

My world belongs to me
If I attempted to explain
What I'm feeling or have felt
Or what I've seen and am seeing
    you'd only receive the crumbs

I am noticing the fire from the sun
The hum in the wind
    storming against my vellus hairs and skin

Intense - just like her love
Extreme - a passion unlike any other
    she chose not to notice the tightness in her grip

I swallowed my resenting words
While her's became deadly war weapons
    heart lacerated and ominously sifted

Puzzling and manipulative
My truth she could not see
    her world belonged to her and mine to me

STAGED

Act 22

I am going to bed now
    and tomorrow I start from scratch

This bed does not belong to me
Nor does this blanket
    and matching sheets

Some time ago - I found a rock way at the bottom
I'm not uncomfortable
My heart is protected
    my thankfulness isn't spoken

The one who controls hears
Without me loosening my lips
I have grieved
    but today I am more content

I forgot my life was uncategorized art
Tomorrow I get to play - have fun and draw
Tomorrow I'll sharpen my pencils
    tomorrow I'll draw a sublime picture

Unearth beauty in all its marks
My head has indented this pillow
    this pillow does not belong to me

I am closing my eyes now
Sleeping for tomorrow
    tomorrow I start from scratch

Act 23

I have a prize that I never won

I have wealth inherited

I protect it
    with intimidating walls made of concrete

Some of this wealth has been stolen - I was naive
    letting crooks get too close

I have wisdom now
    or maybe I have been molded into a cynic

Interrogating your motives because –
my past told me to

This inheritance will not be shared
There is no charity

The stakes are behind the teal of the sky
I am firm
    inflexible and grounded

This richness - sealed and preserved
You will never sing of its tune
    you have never learned the song

Dazzling lamp light beams from the center
You imagine intimacy
I dwell in the authenticity
    the delicacy - of this golden nugget

Act 24

I plucked out the nails you hammered inside
I hoped you would forgive
    and have your perception shift

I was willing and undraped - open and still afraid
The nails gently laid upon the table's drape
I waited - simmering in suspense
Within, I amended my offense
    pledged we'll move forward from this

Silence but no peace - tense

Numbing of my hands
I watched you examine
    the hammer became your fixation

Then you stopped
Your hand relaxed and at your side
Your eyes gaze mine
I'm emotional
    and you - you are stoic

You speak through pounding
With each force I struggle for breath
With each blow I die with you
I never wanted love
    only to mourn my own death

STAGED

Act 25

It persisted through lifetimes
   and with each new being
   it was there embedded in genetic code

Living within subconsciousness
Patterns and sameness
Unknown on levels of awareness
Some were kept still
   and others wanted differences

Those who wanted differences
   urged others tied in blood

They were leaders - fearless
They would embark on missions filled with pride
   rooted in competition

They wanted to champion
They forced their way
Challenges were met
   and progresses stalled

They kept and kept - forgetting to bathe
They aged and naturally withered
   becoming food for earth

Their seeds saw darkness
   until they emerged from fertile soils

A way of remembrance
Mirrored in fragments

STAGED

Again!
And, shed remnants of ancient history
   repeat until fully bathed!

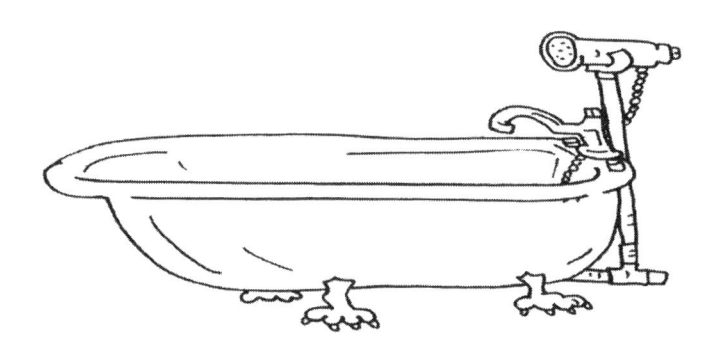

Act 26

Warm me up
I feel a cold coming on
Brew me your best
    simmer it with bliss

Remember how I taught you?
Cover with a lid
Seep and contain the oils
    freeing the steam only to meet our noses

Do you recall our imagination?
Pausing our sentences and moistening our mouths
Mental material was a fathomless landscape
We couldn't answer our whys

We had shoveled and found feverish warmth
Pausing our sentences and moistening our mouths
    we had nothing left to speak of

I noticed the slight bitter on my tongue
Bringing me back to the space we shared
We traveled far in mind but came back with nothing
    and nothing was just fine

STAGED

Silence speaks in rhythms
Waves unnoticed
Telepathic bond
Infinitely expanded
Beyond
My imagination
My comprehension dissolves
Beside the stars - I become silent

STAGED

I am intelligence. My body knows…

Act 27

I am not clever
Everything is up for grabs
I spew gibberish
Laughing at the atmospheric stench

My humor's sense is stubborn and stupid
These fingers are feeble
They have gone limp
Unplugged from the outlet

The room has grown cold and lights have diminished
I took the cup from ol' Joe and drank the backwash
Struggling to remain latched
    hoping for a more robust connection

At least I am in motion - challenges must be felt
Growing at my own cost
Stagnancy is unattractive
    but beautiful when planned

The ugliness emerged years ago
I had deserted the dark ink
Swept away by tremendous tides from life's sea

STAGED

Act 28

What is the sound of silence?
What is the motion in stillness?
Can they coexist?
Many shades of color
    but all came from the same artist

Illusions in names because names differentiate
I would like to believe in my uniqueness
My heart tells inclusions of knowing
    that we are special together

Same as the saltwater in every named ocean

Perfect would be a disservice
Our light never blinds
    instead creates a path of safety

We are loud in silence
Still in the motion
Our world turns and we mingle
Feeling nothing when nothing is everything
    and everything is something

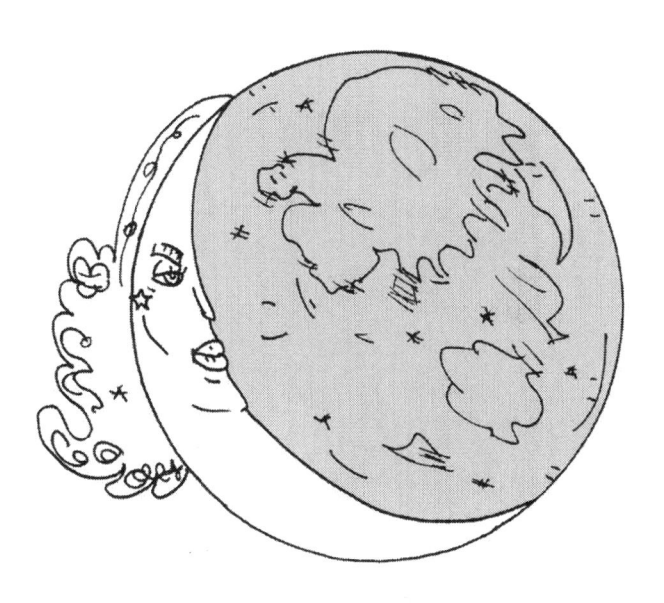

STAGED

Act 29

Once upon a crescent moon
    a girl wanted to roam

Her advisors kissed her forehead
    and told her to be back soon

The girl wandered and made great discoveries
    devouring wild animals and fresh picked wild fruit

Days away from her birth's dwelling
    she started to unwrap freedom

Her advisors were happy but bitter melons

They wanted her to themselves
    but they let go of their powerful hold

Physically

Emotionally

They struggled and made excited at nearby rumbles

Their hearts sobbed and filled with anguish

All they could think of was those farewell kisses
    on their little girl's forehead

Meanwhile, the girl was fast asleep
    after her evening meal - snoring the crescent away

Act 30

My voice vibrated walls of uncertainty
You reflected back my sincerity
I attempted to discover you
    you dodged being seen

Served me pieces of someone else
I couldn't love you
    I loved someone else

The void you feel - I feel it too
I will never have
    what never existed

You were a living ghost - a shy mumble
    unavailable and polar cold

Go ahead and make your puzzle
    I hope you finally see yourself

Judge and blame - thy one at fault
You were never perfect
I admire your war fought
Massive stamina
    your journey bold

Act 31

I noticed that I was out of breath
I decided to sit
I felt content and found that strange
    Hmm

I studied them
Observed their behavior
    how they moved in frantic ways

Moisture coated the rim of my forehead
My tongue coarse like sandpaper
I sipped and swallowed
    life poured into me

Out of the noise - I heard a bird
It distinctively sang
    canceling out the crowd

I smiled
I'm happy sitting here
    for now

Act 32

Ease and effortless
Now I know
I would tug, pull and hold
Causing suffering
    mine alone

I couldn't see past the peaks

My view of me - warped

Compressed

Emotions shrouded - even from self
Wounds bled
I let it drip
    drip, spill and slip

Unremarked
Slowly
Seconds
Moments
Months
Years

Healing arose from its hiding place
    greeting me in warmth

Desperation filled from the inside out - illumination

STAGED

light beamed upon itself

Magnitude of direction
Life with all its
    pain, love and lessons

I couldn't help but grow
Thank you for the Unveiling
Thank you for the Signs
Thank you for the Show
I applaud your Greatness
My heart is soft and receives your Love

Act 33

Bubble burst - exposed
Protection splattered out
Dissolved against the midday's gust
Terror clenches flesh like the tightening of a snake
       against its prey

You become meal - Or else!

Liberate from the prison of hell

Mind turned fiction into memoir
Rereading chapters that were skimmed before
Answers hide in illuminated sight

You chose denial and looked through a blind eye
Compelled by views unseen
       unwitnessed

When will you begin
       to live - beyond the monsters?

Act 34

Realizing that I haven't bowed in completeness
I have had one foot in and one foot out
      but you'd say
      I was covered in completeness

I feel your love encompass my body

I cry

I smile

And, I cry more

You have filed me up once again
      You really do love me

My heart no longer hardened and tight
You give me the freedom to trust
      I bow to you - my Greatest Love

STAGED

Act 35

I am so messy - the kind of messy
    where lukewarm ruby sauce
    takes hostage of my bib

I am so uncaring as my fingers
    playfully dip and paint the walls
    I am not afraid of repercussions
    because there are none

I am learning

Experiencing clarity
The wash of the windowsill

All this perfection
My messiness is perfected
I feel warm inside

My heart released from the squeeze
I cry because I'm overwhelmed
Overwhelmed with your
    full-bodied magical love

All this time - I only had to accept love
Instead of fight against it
I can be really messy
    leaving residues and stains

Act 36

Your brokenness was a bold lie

The inadequacies and judgements made
    were but Stories for sick entertainment

Only to keep you engaged
Only to keep you crazed and caged

It became real - because victimization was your home

You never left it

You continued to decorate
    a home, full of oozing wounds

Act 37

Propelling in the enormity of the unaccustomed
Remembering what fun was
Laughing at the seriousness of my past faces
The humor knots my belly as I recall the stress
    that held suffocating weight

I was immersed and fighting against the current
Unconsciously refusing - a cleanse from debris

All this darkness ahead - I am enthused

The art in my mind is life itself

I am sketching - careful
    of what my additions brings to wholeness

I haven't laughed this loud - wide mouthed

I'd like to be contagious - spreading warm joy
    released from the hellish noise

Act 38

Since you, I don't have much - But more of
    what I had then

This empty room is filled with the morning light
    And happy birds' songs

Amazing what years can usher in and usher out

Swallowed by moments
    never once thinking that they could end

Yet, they surely do
Last night I thought of you

You teach me how to let go
    a Grande gift from God

This well-lit room filled with music
    a Grande gift from God

I smile because I am breathing
The heavy weight of your hand eases
    Now - no longer there gripping mine

I purchased my own royal bed for the first time
I still don't have much - but more of
    what I had then

Fear doesn't bother - peace peaks its head
    and I surrender to a new making of me

Act 39

Thank you for the knowledge
        now I ask you for the way

This knowledge has been indeed useful
        But at times dampens

I'm taught to observe my thoughts
        and I see them clearly in my center eye

They trouble me - one after another
        eager for my attention

Feedback occurs and my body tenses
Pores open and I'm covered with sweat
The rate of my heart increases
I'm aware of what caused this
But my knowledge does not serve me
Only troubles me more because knowledge says
        "you know better"

How many times must I let go and surrender?
Now and every now after
Now and every so often - there are nows
        that I forget to fall
        into wide open loving hands

But now, I remember
        how comforting your hands are
        and how safe I feel held in them
        I'm falling from fear
        thank you for catching me every time I fall

Act 40

Chilling tales of the forbidden river
Most love the spoken suspense
Gossip fills their ears

They'd never attempt to roam
They are safe and free from fear
They laugh from their bellies
    and partake in shared fulfilling meals

Their smiles are contagious
Their hearts radiantly robust

Frail
    the heart of the river

The river speaks in streams
Roars when no one sees
The river is rich and full of itself
Still flows the same direction
    it has - since forever

Act 41

In the morning I gave away my day
Yesterday and the day before I forced
I tried to control what I could not hold in my hands

In the morning - I gently gave up

Now
    it's midday and my heart doesn't pain me as much

I sobbed yesterday and the day before

Today, I remember what simplicity
    and delight feels like

I nurtured my body - filled up on water
My body wanted dark green crisp vegetables
    I slowly chewed

Midday - I was told my eyes were smiling
    my happiness showed

Happiness at times - elusive
Today I held on to it
I know what it's like
    without

Act 42

The current is casually recycling itself through me
I feel the voltage as it forces its way out
I am electric
A ball of vibrant energy

Although - I am not - in awe
I accept my born right mastery
A description full of magical words would be an insult

I am beyond the tricks and spells
    I was once under

Freedom doesn't tease the tip of my tongue
I indulge and I am pleased with the tang

I recall the many moments
    Some - fleeting, I could not keep

And at last
It sacredly lingered
I held tightly to
    goodbye's return

Act 43

Because you wanted to understand - but couldn't
You perceived based on your knowledge
You wanted - but couldn't

Why couldn't you?

You wanted to understand
       what you had already given meaning to

Therefore, you
       satisfied what never needed satisfaction

I was what you had imagined
Anything more or less was absent
I felt smothered
       fogged with the lid covered

You don't see me in my wholeness - but in pieces
I see the whole
       through my brokenness

Act 44

Settle down the noise in my heart
    soften my centerpiece

It's constricted
    in need of swift release

Open my undiscovered treasure
    allow beams to explode

Loosen and relieve
Extinguish the flame
    and wipe away the ash littered in the fire pit

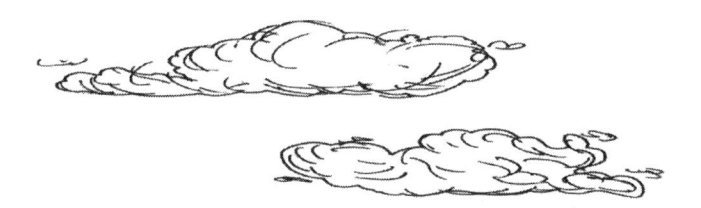

Act 45

Muscles tense - filled with memories of emotion
They feel painful with every subtle move
Torched when touched
My thoughts lie in frozen time
        scattered among thickened ice

My mind remembers
        and my body re-enacts the script

For how long?
Years old - consider it classic

This artful creation - left crumbs and residue
Parts of me fell into trance
Hypnotic concoction of slow dramatic death
The glass was full
        and I unknowingly gulped
            until a slight layer of poison settled at the very bottom

Bloated with toxins
Terribly undetected
Life seen through kaleidoscopes
        the source of toxic load
            uncovered because of the rapid wind

The drape fell violently - But I hoarded and protected

The weight was far too dangerous
        for those winding roads

STAGED

Why didn't I let go?
Because it was all I had
       and all I had ever known

Act 46

The clouds colored gray - water rang
    coating before the absorption in cracked soil

We worried we'd never peel fruit again

During the starve - I resented

My stomach empty on air
My chapped skin coarse like wee rocks meshed in clay
Mist accompanied whistling and howling wind

We slaughtered
We sacrificed to lie still without chill
    wrapped in beast skin

Miracles made ash and smoke
Miracles gave rain and brought it to halt
Comfort in the miracle of soil and tears
Comfort I could peel the bitter layer

    Swish the juices
    spit away the seeds

STAGED

Act 47

Illusions filled the pockets of mind
        loose change meant nothing

Reality felt real but only known to you
Designs reimagined
        after times of stall

Sameness was the pseudo safety

Illusions differ from yours
Basic is beautiful but basic is Grand
The mind built steel walls for protection
        there was never any danger

There were never any complexities
        it was all just entertainment
        a moment of rhythmic dance
        combined in Parental Love

The most outstanding

Mimic the traits - all encompassing
        sowed into the fabric
        inescapable

Latched in the adhesive of web
Life lived inside Earth - The Womb

Act 48

Purple hearts - spilled love all across
It was the purist

Maybe because
    these purple hearts encountered
    tainted love and worked earnestly
    to never possess such fragmented
    distorted love

Purple hearts intensely feel
Purple hearts tread from the shallow
Pursuing meaning while questioning

Purple hearts are
    curious
    afraid
    but courageous

They long for trust and understanding

Purple hearts have a mighty pound
    a result from the resistance endured

Act 49

Here I am in my shell
My vehicle
My avatar
I am detached although I feel the
        cracks
        the clash
        and see my animations

There is an emptiness
I try to enjoy this unique experience
        but as of now I feel no fulfillment

Source must delight in their sense of humor
These birds chatter and I - wonder why
These squirrels have given me
        the most mysterious stare
        as if they have read my mind
        or tapped into my vibrational speech

Some say

"Don't question, you will never rejoice in an answer."

But I can't help myself
I've forced and given up
Both haven't done much good

I'm a bitter melon - tanging up my own tongue
This shell
This vehicle
This avatar

STAGED

has been pushed with the sailing wind
and God has written it so

Act 50

There was no cheer among any lively crowd
There was a lonesome score only I could count
I felt defeated as my score depleted
Losing - while only I, could see it

    "Pity me" my mirror says

And the Forces
    the ones that take pride in all your pain
    and failure
    they laugh until they cry
    drooling at the free feed of energy served
    a plate of lifeless slob

They have gratitude and they rejoice

I have lost but these rounds are in trillions
Before - I played without knowing
But how could I now know
    yet, still stupidly lose
    they are experienced –
    but I'm finally catching up

This loss is better than the ones before
Their old-fashioned tricks are not so hidden anymore

I aim for target
They danced around my sharp arrow
    and I missed

Subtle in their approach

STAGED

I'll want to play again
This time I'm prepared - more than I've ever been
They take violently
Only if I allow
See, now
    I laugh when we play around
    because I'm winning
    my plate is being served now
    filling up selfishly
    feasting
    taking what's mine and has always been

They want my heart
They want my spirit
They hate my happiness

The
    Sadness
    Fear
    Sickness
    and despair
    Is what they hope for - the most

My goal is to keep what rightfully belongs to me
    my heart
    my spirit
    my happiness

Act 51

You bantered and I gave a sided smirk
You blamed me of seriousness
You must think I am rigid
Perceptions unreliable
I'm neither flexible nor rigid
I am just behaving in a way
    where I - only see a landing place

Pure focal points
Maybe I'm seeing passed you
I see you - but I know this moment is transient
I scanned the connection
    and figured
    the trivial talk had meaning only of interference

Swayed - but I have not fallen
Thoroughly rooted in my Grandness
That may be hard for some to understand
The shift is happening as we speak

Aboard - you have time because it will never leave

I am here
You didn't meet me
You met peace

Act 52

As a child I grew up with many treasure hunts
I searched for something
It couldn't be named
        but I earnestly explored

My heart open and magnetic
But nothing ever stuck
I was spoiled but wanted more
        because I was told I should have it

There was the unconditional that never changed
Then there was the superficial - fleeting
Superficial messages
        dominated aged Sony tube screens

Most times
        the stories told weren't a reflection of me

Yet
        the stories still penetrated my subconscious

I should find love one day
I should find that treasure of fortune
I should rebel against all odds of me being the lesser
I should compete
        until we lie in dry blood and broken teeth

Act 53

You showed up again
last time we weren't ready

Maybe it's all fun for you
Maybe I think this
because
I had fun with hearts
      while they formed a bruise

When will my karma be returned?

How can I give my heart
      when I am afraid to taste my own poison?

I don't trust you
      because - I don't trust myself

You are the pain I tried to run away from
      but I always wanted

I dreamt of us - too many times
      even when I shouldn't have

You and I both - slaughter hearts
      We kill love

We are pricked by the rose's thorns
      but still want a whiff of its sweet scent

STAGED

      take me
where I have never been
surprise me with nothing

Act 54

Rocks of earth
Pavement of man
Feet of authority

A chill fallen - braised my ankles
Dreaded steps snatching away Velcro

It wasn't permanent - I had to use strength

Forgotten pennies
        the bronze much darker

Black chewing gum lay beside someone's free dresser

Tall can - sipped
        empty canned beers littered

Cigarette butts and bird's shit

Tires skid
        spun then stopped

You may not remember
I am certain you do not
I cannot remember your face
        because I only saw your feet

Only moments after what you had told me
        I began to see the skyscrapers
        electrical poles
        planes and sea sky

STAGED

You saved me when my spirit pleaded to die
        encouraged me - you, a stranger
        I'll never forget your deed
        I hope you are well
        I'll continue to look up
        away from the blacken chewing gum

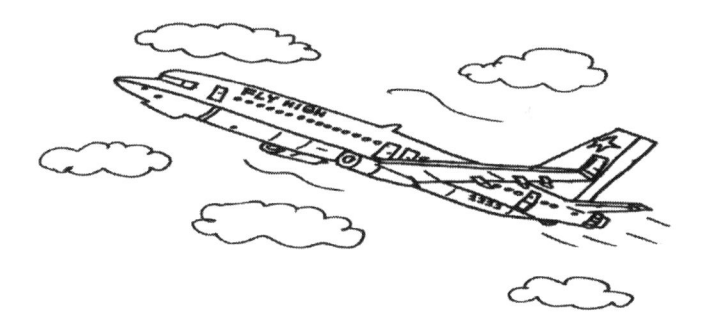

Act 55

i weep and my tears turn into welts

i do not have to have a reason - to have felt

the massive swiveling tornado - twisting away at my heart

i am a storm of disguise

my face does not say it all

please do not assume my joy

STAGED

I sang with the ocean's rhythm
I let the wind smooch my toffee skin
I gave away my worries
In exchange for safety and hope
I filled up on wisdom
While my feet soaked the simmered sand

Act 56

Your cheer doesn't sound like joy
    but piercing pain
    you altered your reality and welcomed spirits
    you covered up the damage dormant within

Escape and find freedom – temporarily
    only to come back down to the same low

Dignity - I wish portrayed
    but you've brought me down
    along for your drunken ride
    not cutting of cars but source's supply

You startle and do not care
Your fun - a celebration of damage
Inconsiderate and selfish
    wake the neighbors with your ignorance

I see me in you
    the me
    I've been out of breath running from
    forgive me, for I have judged
    I have complained and broke out in hives

Either way this bounce is filled with ill health
We affect each other indirectly
    I'd like to ruin your gathering
    tape each mouth shut
    all in the name of peace

STAGED

I am disturbed by your
>howls, chatter and pseudo screams
>over the stars laughter
>they can hear you up there

My peace threatened
What does that say about me?
>I am rejecting you
>and concurrently rejecting me

There's room in this world for both of us
I stalled to remind myself
Too caught up in flames
>gassed from anger

This illusion shall pass
Many lessons from every corner
I am aware of the triggers - living in the triggers
Loving myself is a duty while soaked in them

Before I would have succumbed
Spent some money and became one
>with the madness

Forgive me for I have harbored judgement
>in my angered heart

I'm letting go of what I want - accepting what is
>in this obnoxious moment
>>I intend to sleep tonight
>>dream to recover in productivity
>>I observe the distractions
>>I see myself in them
>>I have judged myself

Act 57

You are troubled and no one knows
Your heart misused as a punching bag
How many times?
    Enough to never break again

Sorrow is not my comfortable bed where I laid
I would go back trillions of instances to tell you
    you were loved

You deserved more and less of cruel wars
    but now your heart has shriveled and dried
    it struggles to pump but it still manages

No one gave you credit
    and they didn't have to
    only you could give such recognition
    to the battles won

I have not seen a soldier like you
    you have lived through death
    you are more than able to tell your story
    through your stroll

You can withstand the whips
    and cursing on your spirit

I have never seen - a soldier like you
It isn't in me to admire and gaze so intensely
    but you
    you are my magnet
    I'm only reflected by you

STAGED

I am imagination…

Please take a moment to indulge at our concession stands. If you have to use the restroom, please do so now while we are in intermission…

Act 58

Hold your spirit
Take care to how you feel
Elevate when in spaces of
      regret, loss and sourness

Composure comprised in mind
      I cannot be swung
      when there is no playground

I laugh because
      you are caught up
      in your own game - child

I see your neediness and wailing for attention
      I am amused

Entertained in how you have behaved
I examine - because it is my nature
I am inclined to notice the subtle
      sneaky and scheming - you have many toys
      manipulation
      lies
      vengeance with no recipients

My compassion is growing
There may be reasons you are the way you are
      background of loud noises from your past
      they trickle outwards

Maybe you don't even notice the pain anymore
It's become your normal

STAGED

Or has this always been your normal?
Did someone strip away at your innocence?
Did you begin to see the world of agony?

You couldn't find an escape
Pleasantly comfortable
any other way - was an arduous task to undertake

I cannot help you
I can only help myself
My compassion is a seedling
My peace isn't disturbed
      I hope to love you
        the way I should love myself

Act 59

Smoke filled the air causing alarm
Strangers awkwardly wiggle feet apart from them
Their heads tilted and faced the sidewalk

The others' dinner is heating up on a makeshift pit
Strangers never acknowledged
The presence of another human's life

They felt fear
Why did they feel fear?

Ignored
Left
Forgotten
Stigmas and assumptions

Our worldly siblings
    some suffer in broad day
    filling up on poison
    scarred wicked art forearms

Be upset with the poison
    but the poison isn't true for some
    the truth was the hindrance of circumstances
    circumstances created strategically

Some have mental power and aren't fallen prey
Some have scruffy kneecaps
    from the sincerity - in how they have prayed

They must

STAGED

otherwise, they crumble like rocks in canyons
unseen
unremembered
it never happened
they don't exist

Act 60

Hope fell from my pocket - I carelessly littered
    it was safe where it was once kept

Hope doesn't mean much these days
    I outgrew the hopes
    I outgrew the desire
    of one day having you
    when you became ready

Patience made me a fool
    Laugh - and I would understand

The fantasies I entertained
    while calling someone's else's name
    I am guilty
    of being the very bad joke

Naive

How could I succumb to a hunter
    and become catch?

I let go of lust and regret
    I let you flow down stream

You've become a lesson
    the knowledge written
    on the walls of my heart

STAGED

Act 61

Can you see me or am I invisible?
Am I not what you wanted?
Did I rid your assumptions?
Or will I remain what you created

There are stereotypes sketched upon me
    I didn't pen them there

I feel the pressure of just being
    Caught between
    what you would expect from me
    and what I actually am

I have spent my life proving - I am as dry as bone
    empty as the desert's pond

You see flesh
    and all the names given to it
    you have never seen me for who I am
    because
    you have never seen yourself

Etiquette - I have none and I don't care
Systems functioning
    and I opt out because
    they are beyond repair

The herd left me lonely
But my lonesome
gave me muscles that never tear

STAGED

My strength has already moved the mountains
        and rearranged the moon
          the Universe is my living room

I dwell and take up space
        I will not be down soon
        My head floats above
        Lost in the oblivion

I stare at fear and - I become enraged

My deepest breath fails to dispel ego
        And your ego
        has pulled you away from me
        so in division I observe

        The illusion

Death has struck me many times
I wonder the point in games of life

Why?

Peace has no enthusiasm or cheer - we crave
        Greed
        Violence
        Attacks
        Envy
        Like chilled copper blond beer

ACT 62

Tint shade of nuisance

Slick - slipping pass

Caught hammock swinging and smirked face

Minimalism detected the outburst unheard

Without calm
    you wouldn't distinguish the rumble

Swaying like a building of twelve floors

I felt the quake

The attack made

Fire extinguished
    with the purity of water

Become wave - wave wiped out the entirety

    Fire tamed

Characters develop as the plot progresses…

ACT 63

I want to watch you write
Analyze your mind
    see how easily it comes
    or how you struggle finding words

Invite me to the intimacy
Of your delicate pen
    mind and lonely page
    allow me to be entertained
    As I sit and stare
    at creations becoming in full bloom

Rays of sunshine ignite
A storm of lightning - all at the same time

What a show

You pour out until empty - stalled
    but you become full again
    mind raced and won the page
    quickly turning to the other
    replicating images only seen by you

Gemstones scatter your pages

Dazzling glow of aura
    settles atop your opened book
    of sacred notes

Intimate - what a radiant show

ACT 64

You are a part of the grandness
I should have an opened heart
I should love you despite your jagged rock of a heart

I breathe deep to heal
I breathe deep to consume life
You are life and many more exhibit the same traits

I feel I am not alike
Reality viciously peels the veil
And I see me behind you

I see pain - a sobbing heart
      oozing wounds

I had to develop compassion for myself
I now extend it to you
I will not curse you
Or cover you in dirt

You have every right to be Grand
My world opens to yours
Yours to mine

They are the same in every way
I hear your cries
And I loudly hear mine

Somehow - I smile
I am thankful for you
Thankful for your lessons

STAGED

You are my muse
My teacher
My reflection

ACT 65

Expected a fragile heart to turn bold
Fragments leaked slippery warm blood
Hope shed light yay high
Dispersed and fleeting

Hearts struggle to open
Lies became an unsettling truth

Where is my wholesome honesty?

I have forced - and therefore have not moved
This reality only known by me
      caused shivers as I laid in bed to sleep

We only want love
Love from what we seek

What have I gained from my attempts?
      fragments leaking slippery warm blood

Self-negligence

Accustomed to hiding
Accustomed to adapting - for you
Not for the one whose eyes are moist

Heart terrified and disabled
      self needs affection
          the kind that is Not - for anyone else

ACT 66

Safe behind screens
But your mind is not
Subtle shifts from glances
Defend your wellbeing at all cost

What is life lived with a mind lost in apparitions?

You have not seen my truth
I have never seen yours
This snapshot of a portrait isn't real
    just like your desires
        a foggy cloud a foot away from the ground
        you could hike through without noticing

Stoned stare - aimless steps

But don't be too serious
    unloose your button and unstrap your belt
    sit for a while
    abandon the clock and focus on breath

You have done so already
    it didn't help
    quiet, shhh - never tell
    the agony hidden behind the veil

I am made of love from intelligence…

ACT 67

Deceived only because
    I believed in you

What you gave
    was only to receive attention

It was bait and I unwisely bit it
    there is value

Me not being wise ironically gave me wisdom

I played with a torch's fire
    and I sculpted the flame

You came as a beautiful teacher
    I only know it now

You said that lessons aren't in everything
Yet, I gained knowledge profound
We danced on the water's surface
You gave me reason to dive down

Otherwise, I might have grown stagnant
Repeatedly kicking up wave

Truth swam with the hoax
Side by side there for interpretation
I'm intrigued still
    even after the class
    you didn't know you taught

ACT 68

I lost myself in sorrow
years turned into minutes
I watched them pass by
      by the second

I wasn't so attentive
      displaced in the fluff of cloud

Filled with losses - experiences I wished for
      remain certainly a wish
      they are no longer here

Only energy - transformed into oneness
At times I can feel my
      heart wrapped tightly in love
      other times I'm so distant
      captured in worldly naps

How can I be so distant when the love is here within?

How do you feel when someone leaves abruptly?
      some ends never meet
      and questions never get answered
      peace may not lie in the why
      rather in the acceptance

I cannot have what I would like and that's okay
      It's okay because maybe we'll meet again
      after the last page of my book
      when there's nothing left to read
      slip into an infinite slumber - unworldly

ACT 69

I can't call your name - you don't have one
I can't see your face
    It's turned red
    and covered in rain

The drops extinguished the flames - now you shiver

You withdraw
You want cures and you want calm

Clutter clenches curves
Your mind overburdened and wild
You gave name to your trauma
Demons sprint and attack
No warning

You find solace as your head tilts
Your lips open to whisper
A plea for help

Faded thoughts like handed down denim
The bright became dim
    and your mind's lantern
        finally blew after thousands of blows

But you are strong
    you open jars on the first squeeze
    pop and sizzle
    because you are strong
    but not strong enough

STAGED

Forgotten wounds silently sound
        the darkest tune dances
        out of rhythm
        the lyrics sing
        "I am strong"
        in repetition

ACT 70

You've hidden your diary
It wasn't mine for casual reading
You folded it up so neatly - wrapped in leather string
Packed inside a wooden drawer

Slowly it slid closed - It reminds me of your heart
    forbidden and mysterious

But I'm mischievous
My hands made me do it
I can't define trust
Boundaries are invisible

I am not to blame
It called in the night
    when the moon lit the room

I befriended your heart
    you'll never know

I am, a project of Mind…

STAGED

ACT 71

My mind created you
You sat at the edge of my heart
I thought of you too many times
Space was filled with memories
       of what you and I were

But we never were

You said to me how you were afraid
       I wanted to save you

Now I want all of you
       but we're both stupidly
       standing in the way

Beautifully complicated

My insecurities tell me
       I'm not the only one
       being deeply stared upon

I wish you would let me all in
       you did - and I missed it
       my heart secretly sobs
       sometimes you're here
       and other times you're not
I'll never forget the magic we made
       a muse that's followed me for eons

You have given me insight

Connection surpassed us
        this connection led to discoveries
        of me
        finding myself

STAGED

ACT 72

Pour me full before I collapse of thirst

I spun dizzy in thoughts

Grew tired runnin' after you

You stop or walk? I can't tell

My past has gripped me
and created a cloud of disbelief

Why do I feel so caught?

This doesn't exist and I know it

I forgot this was all an illusion

My heart doesn't *really* smile for you

I never wanted it - my match made on earth

I am hopeless - romantically hopeless

Cynical and sorry

Lingering and afraid

ACT 73

Glory outshined the humbled
The key was held disgustingly selfishly
Conscious lies carefully chewed
      acidic and regurgitated

Oh, the privilege assumes innocence
She wouldn't swat a fly to diminish the irking buzz
      Monsters do not hide

Everyday encounters
Misleading slow creep
Has their heart
      become a sinking hole filled with debris?

Safety safely exited - away from the humbled
The humbled left
      to fend on their accord

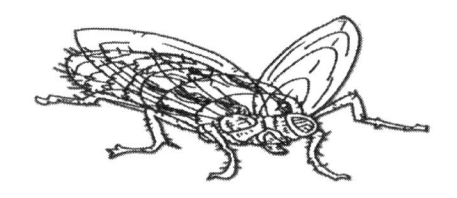

ACT 74

Do you believe in
> fate
> destiny
> accidents
> coincidences?

What's the meaning behind the words?

Is there all or is there nothing?

Is there something nested in the middle?

Even when you see nothing - you are seeing something

What is my sigh?

My heart beats
> I never once put in effort
> my cuts heal from Your magic eraser

I am no fun
> simple talk distracts me
> politics - a game board
> and I am no fan of dice

You let us run wild - while foam forms at our mouths

Who filled Me with
> greed, anger, envy, hate and Jealousy?

STAGED

Meanwhile
> tsunamis and quakes
> drown and fracture
> bullets rip skin and stings the core of flesh

Have you no remorse?

Your school

I'll never know
> when you'll ring the bell
> many before having heard it rang
> they left here - some afraid
> some content
> but all were brave

ACT 75

Pieces plagued your deceived heart
You became emotional all because of parts
Sworn fully that truth was what you saw

A new connection arose - bridging gaps
Only on the surface with miles long slithering cracks
Isolation excreted from below
Lonely and insecure
Propelled yet, lost

Images of what is acceptable
    but you've never quite fit inside that mold

The world has lost its mind
Placing value where there is none
Counterfeit
Mirages and tricks
    the World's offer

Madly falling in love with items
    they contain nothing

Madly falling in love with praise
Chasing forever while True Love fades shaded grey

How many strings conduct this body?
    too many I couldn't count

At times I rather delve in

STAGED

Consume all until I'm completely burdened
Outpouring ignorance
Step in line and cower
Believe in their language
Believe in their religions
Believe in their roles they have created for me
       I am their creation
       sadly

Who takes the pride and responsibility in this art?

I am someone's image
       But I never wanted to be
       intently painted this way

I rebel in thought
I am not what I ought - So I think

Am I really free?

Poisonous prison planet
       privacy pry
       plethora of outspoken lies

Act 76

My tea brews - slowly simmering
Emotions gather
The ones familiar
I have collapsed to knees
Drenched in the saltiest seas

I once forgotten to swim with elegant strokes
Fear concocted with despair
No longer bounds me in containment

I stood
       then wiped my knees of the debris
       brought in from the outside

I am bothered by my shift

       How could I have traveled so far and end up where I longed for?

Bothered, rattled and shaken
       Awakened

Meeting me anew
This introduction came sudden
Finally arrived
       and started seeing someone completely new

How do I manage this change
       and gracefully sit where I am placed?

Everyone said to go and get there

STAGED

They never once mentioned
>the overwhelming celebration of love

Salty waters - bright blue
>happiness washes my heart
>>cleaning all emotions that no longer serve

Birth is beautiful but living wholly
>has task and responsibility

I carefully write this chapter - in front of my eyes
>blank pages fill without me lifting a pen
>>I have finished and now I am creating again
>>>this time on purpose

Act 77

Bound by blood but we don't match
These self-inflicted wounds
We have grown very much accustomed to
    they are in plain sight

It was a mirror I glimpsed last night
Reminders of pain that haunts
    the deeply rooted and difficult to pluck

These chains are made by a sturdy brand
    a brand that taught us
    to slowly hate each other
    the brand of oppression

Slashed so deeply - our skin ripped open
    wide and hot pink

We don't like what we see
We tear down ourselves
While tearing down one another
    Oh, I am saddened by our ways

I begged of love - empty hands came
Oh, this world of shivers
I pray for healing over my blood

Dispel the insidious infections
Diminish generational curses
Allow us to love
Allow forgiveness
    and a shining light of compassion

Gather costumes from the enormous wardrobe.
A generous amount is made available for everyone.

Act 78

Guilt doesn't possess me like a surviving ghost
My heart no longer attacks itself like autoimmune

My heart discovered order
Now lounging in calm waters

My heart - as free as my neighbor's feather
Roaming in air

I own this moment
My peace is not leased

It is something I have when I let go of the squeeze
    released

My emotions congregate
    befriending each other

I am their host, and we all know

guilt - isn't welcomed here

STAGED

I am the keeper of fortune
This fortune cannot be earned
It is inherent

Act 79

Tasting reality
Activating the sensors of my mind
Smoke scattered the sky
Ashes fell like snowflakes
Irritating my eyes

Day became darkened
The sun vanished
Morning became filled with fear
    and mourning

Taken for granted
    what our Great Mother provides
        perfect streams and attractive blue skies

I feel content
It was written like this
Messages sent from something Greater
Affecting more than me - a transfer of I to We

But I feel content
Observing within - my lack of emotion
My contentedness feels nothing
And no thing is - freedom

My heart doesn't ache
Many before me succumbed
Those I didn't know
    and those that were dearly close

STAGED

Most find justice in fighting for life
        death is the only thing certain

So, if the flames decide to spread
        turn me into beige sand
        let me be casually walked over
        let me be the wisdom in the land

Unbothered

Strangely content

Many disasters
        calamity and calamity
        lightning bolts
        rain halts
        but it was written

Our Great Mother Loves and Scolds
Rewarding and taking away
Be grateful
        and behave
        she says

Act 80

I met a millionaire once
    he paced the floor
    carrying his valuables

I looked him in his eyes - I could see his dreams
He didn't speak much
    avoiding others
    making sure not to
    impede on their paths

I met a millionaire once
Carefully, he kept
    his valuables in close sights

From his eyes, I caught the glance
    of the dream in his mind

He defined himself
    away from where everyone else slept

    Scattered pages and newspapers
        covered his bed like blankets

        Surely, he was there
        but someplace else

Act 81

Listen attentively
See beyond words fallen from strangers' lips
Widen your gaze
Let attention overcome you

Lately you've noticed but ignored
Please ignore no longer
Guidance is with you
       guidance has been there all around
       like the forgotten air you breathe

Sickened by fear and uncertainty
Faith dismantled from circumstances unwanted

You chose to ignore - to be uneducated

       Do you not remember options?

       Do you not remember impermanence?

For every problem a solution rest
       a pause waiting on you to play
       disconnected while everything
       is in its place
       waiting for you to resume
       In your Grand Game

Life of surprises
Random turns
Lessons waiting to be found and learned
Opportunity is there

STAGED

Where it has been – never once hiding
You've hid yourself
>   choosing to look away from the subtleties
>   whispers are faint

The apparent was difficult to comprehend
>   let go to pay attention
>   waking up
>   only to try - once again

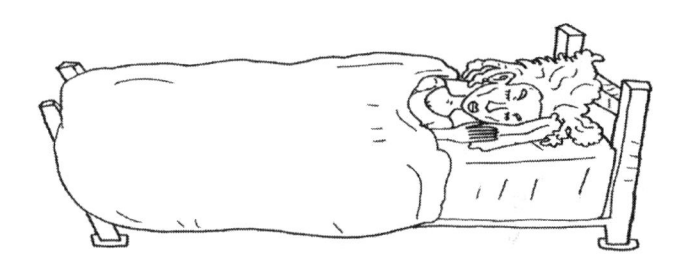

Act 82

Full
Satisfied
What you provided I perceive as magic

        Is anything too difficult?

        Was there any effort involved?

We have all grown
I didn't notice my sprout
I just see me in the here and now
    Full

My inner workings mechanical - you made it that way
    and I am lazy
    I just lay
    breathing in and out
    what I have taken for granted

I can taste the breeze
    coming in from the outside
    your intelligence put it there

My eyelids cover my sight
I'm seeing black, pink and white
    your intelligence
    made my projections

My feet feel clammy and cold
    as my heels sink into the mattress

STAGED

My hands hold nothing but air
My thoughts resemble yours
       Creatively

Your hands empty of wands
I am your thought aware of itself
My eyes drench in awe

Magnificent birth

       Do you feel prideful?

Standing ovation for seeds smothered in soil
I bow to you and your Greatness
I consume your Creations
My heart speaks

       Do you feel my thankfulness?

STAGED

Act 83

Chaos casually creeped in unwelcomed
The people became ill across our earth
There was a panic
        deep seated denial and
        whiffs of sadness in the air
        along with thick smoke
        filling lungs of the wrinkling old
        young - dreamy and innocent

The mask we wear now
        don't compare
        to the minuscule mask back then
        Young child, life was a lot different
        Mountains sang and our seasons
        were in the beginning stages
        of not being seasons at all - much like now

Young child, it pleases me
        to witness how you live off the land that's left
        it comes naturally
        sweetheart, I hadn't the slightest clue

I had to learn quickly to fend for myself
        I saw sweet peace
        turn into hatred and war - between neighbors
        violence struck the spirits
        of those most religious

Masks weren't *really* mask at all back then

Act 84

You're troubled and no one knows
Your heart misused as a punching bag

How many blows?
        enough to never break again

Sorrow isn't my comfortable bed where I laid
        I'd go back trillions of instances
          just to tell you that you were loved
          you deserved more love
          and less of the cruel wars

Now your heart is swiveled and dry
        wary and untrusting
        callus and deadened

Rereading the same script
Without intent to edit

The pain is like a limb
        a part of you
        that without it
        you'd feel like something - was missing

Identities change
There are possibilities in the stories you tell
No one is listening except for you

Only you, only you - are accepting the ache
        as if - liberation was just as fictional
        as the stories you create

Act 85

No bitter on my sun drops
Kisses make the rain stop

I see me in a beautiful land
Covered in love so pristine

You couldn't -
meet me halfway

The sun met me fully

The sun -
offered me comfort

I finally felt seen

Act 86

I don't want to go but I'm obligated
Cold turning warm bronze chain
Nothing in sight to break it
Knees and hands painted in dirt

        Crawling towards what exit?

Swung 'round like a child's toy
I am human - and I have a mind

My efforts well intended - but
        my heart doesn't make music

The joy of sound - something distant
They have thrown me scraps
Mush and mold grown

This anklet
        the jewelry of misery

I see the moon's reflection
I see mine too

Pleasant tunes
        won't sweetly sing
        all I have is hope
        the hope to hear
        the instrument inside me play

Act 87

The sun set on my eyelids
The birds' chirps were music from a language
        unknown

The air blew through my cracked window
        it smelled like
        Saturday morning

I yawned and stretched pulling the
        cotton threaded sheet
        and heavy blankets away

My heart filled with love and thankfulness
        choices I choose from
        will guide my day

Today, I will be intentional
        alert and amused
        by this life's offering

STAGED

Act 88

Fooled by my own sight
If I suffer something finds it humorous
While I find it appalling

    How could you set this in my pathway?

I've just stumbled out of breath to get here
    I saw the mountain
      Honestly, I was intimidated

I just knew it was *only* a strenuous climb
Many told me different routes to take
I chose my mind and set my intuition aside

Prepping with fear and anxieties
    I became - bold
    I treaded
    ascending
    drinking up pride

My pores spilled water
I began to feel confident and strong
Listening to the crackles of my feet
    against the fallen leaves

Feeling the pain of sharpened rocks
Noticing the beauty
    of waist high plants
    and hidden nest

STAGED

The sky colored with Falcons - I made the most noise
The silence offered me reflection and - time
        wasn't counted for

Only a few more steps
The higher I reached - the wind became angry
        causing me to sway

The wind's forceful resistance led me
        to question my determination

I did not give in
I too, became angry - fighting with the wind

Finally, I reach
This time not drinking up pride
        but swallowing the reality
        that I would have to repeat - this
        many - times

Many massive mountains
I think I know the land
I know what it has taught me

My intuition tells me
        to rest on the smooth beige rock

I sit and prepare
        The wind now whispers
        and tells me
        "I never prepare, I'm just here"

Act 89

Streetlights and a cold porch
Brewed steaming tea cools
Alone - with the morning and thoughts

I have become her

My child eyes watched
        as she sat snugged in the dark
        sipping and sighing

Her thoughts spoke out
Worries scattered forth

I could hear the lighter flick
        once and then again - flicking

I could smell the smoke
Floating through the screen doors

Through my window - I could hear her thoughts
Her moment of serene
        by herself
        in wee hours

Act 90

My exhale reminds me
That it is time to let go
I have been soaring in the sky - for miles
      I am diving down
      back to earth's soil

Faith renews me
The soil soothes - I plunge deeper
      bathing in the beautiful mud

My tears rained down from above
      and splashed me with hope

Refreshed with a sought-after smile
It has been at a shy distance for quite a while now

My aches dissolve
Tension transformed
Loosening and opening up

I give away
Because what I have been holding
I cannot keep

I feel a growth spurt - It is inevitable

Magic happens in Earth's soil
      I have been planted here for a reason
      The reason may be unknown
      But the unknown is - synonymous
      with faith

STAGED

ACT 91

Five minutes train delay - we wait
Strangers glance
Time like a wild sloth

My eyes intrigued by people
    and the stories they contain
    I'm curious
    but I'm shy
    I watch as dialogues recite

Wheels screech in the distance
    it becomes louder
    we stand in line
    like kindergartners

        Welcome on board
        Please stand clear of the doors

We roam for seating
    I saw this woman
    she held onto her walker
    talking to a gentleman
    in kind conversation - he seemed
    uninterested

She confided
    telling pieces of her story
    spinal surgeries
    and arthritic hand pains
    the gentleman nodded and said

STAGED

                "mmhmm"

Paying attention to his third arm
Screen light lit his eyes, she asked

                "what do you do?"
And
                "where are you from?"

His replies short and to the point

                "sales, Houston."

The gentleman styled in shined brown loafers
       suited for his life

The woman looked forward to a warm bath
The gentleman looked forward to his flight
Gap of wisdom hovered over

I wonder what else she could have offered
I wonder what the gentleman sales
Opportunities of connectedness

Strangers speak - on surface

She at least tried to dive in three feet deep

She exited the train

I hope her bath was warm - like she wanted

ACT 92

The storm started after sunset
Whooshing thunder and a wind party
Rain tumbled down from the sky
    scattered the terrain in jewels
    startled with light
    beams lighting up
    the blackened sky

Sparkling and drizzled
Many jewels chipped - creating mosaics
Eyes fell in deep love with the art of nature
The finest beauty one could ever witness
The storm was complete
    despite the segmented
    jewel droplets

Sacred stones danced in the spotlight
    a celebration of storm
    It's raining
    and pouring out like
    Yosemite waterfalls

Shimmering sparkles of a magic trick
The secrets,
    forever unknown

Act 93

Mustard yellow with texture
    your eyes rest in kaleidoscopes

Perplexed
    I am

Perception
    that belongs to you

        How did it shape that way?

Defenses - I can sense the repulsion

Mustard yellow with texture
    your eyes rest in the telescope
    facing the moon

I am - just because
    stripped with nothing
    to prove

I was broken
    maybe that shows
    but those are just reruns
    displayed on the screen
    of my soul

I read you like a life assignment
    our comprehension
    below average

STAGED

Pigeon grey pecking at dry bread

Perception
    that belongs to me

Time could have taught
    But it was fleeting
    like the sun after the evening

You still chase the moon
    hoping to trigger your senses
    with its texture

I was there like early morning fog
    but swept away and forgotten
    you knew nothing at all

Your eyes rest in kaleidoscopes
    I am the mustard yellow
    with texture

To someone else I may be
    earthly teal

I am pulsating in every color
    but what you see is factual
    I have no control over your beliefs
    I am art
    stroked with a brush
    from a hand
    that knows more than us

ACT 94

I wonder the conversations
       beneath the earth
       the trees have seen many
       arrive and leave

Their roots strong
       and weave creating art unseen
       you don't know wisdom
       like them

Their stillness teaches
       and their beauty is to live for

Fallen golden leaves
       become home to concrete
       I wonder if the branches
       miss them

We live in corrupted wild
       receiving tainted portions
       unless we travel to wild
       named by men

It's easy to get lost - waiting at the red light
       anxiously anticipating
       our day at the job

We see blinkers
       read billboards
       and signs
       for the entrance of the freeway

STAGED

Rushing and honking

Angry - for what?

Dismissing the portions
> we have
> because responsibilities
> drive throughout the freeway

I'd like to travel the freeway
Immersed in autumn air
Free
> like roots stretching miles

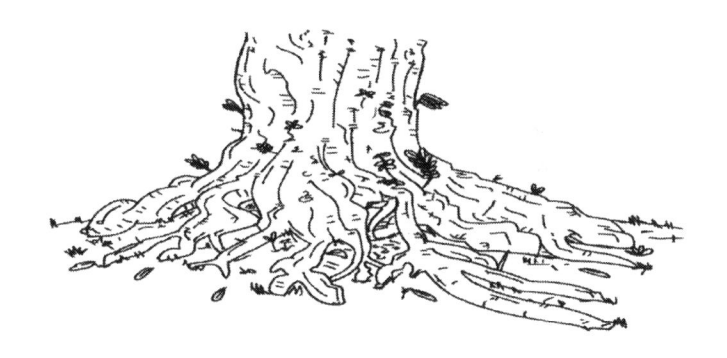

Act 95

They wanted forever in a moment
    souls mating
    souls separating

We closed our eyes, and our forever wasn't real

I loved on conditions
I never accepted you - for you

You clung and I bounced around in space
    living in passed lost loves
    and heartbreaks

I wanted what you could not offer
I stayed anyway
    watching you grow
    and succeed

Your adaptability
    and intelligence
    always intrigued me

I loved you in a special way - friends cuddling
    kissing
    and playing house
    a few years - too long
    happy family
    raising a cat and dog

Your aggression - passive
Mine - expressive

STAGED

I needed time to think

You needed time with me
    and reassurance
    for everything

I hope we remember what we gained
    and never take for granted
    the night we met

Family goes and so does friends
    but lessons are taught
    in the end

Our goodbyes - an exchange of knowledge

Act 96

What is it that you need?
You keep checking
but every time you look it's still there

Either take or calmly sit

You behave spoiled
Once you get
You want more

I could splash the ocean on you
       and you would still complain of the sun

I could place the moon
       and you would complain of the winter's cool
       and how your little hands and fingers numb

You wanted protection and I provided

Joyously

You wanted a bed
       and now you just lay there - and think

What do you need?

I watch you sob
       when you have everything

I've given you the script
       maybe you forgot your lines

STAGED

I've given you your Stage
       yet your character is off

I want you to relax and be nothing at all

No script
No direction
Sleep
       and then
       we
       can talk

STAGED

I only name the nameless
for my understanding

The nameless
doesn't yearn
to be
understood

Act 97

I watch you lie like staring myself in a mirror

Familiarity struck me
    like cold water
        on my face in the morning

I find humor in myself

What does that say about someone
    who laughs at themselves?

Now giggling at you
    with you
        both of us comics

But do you laugh at your own jokes
    or am I the only attendee at your show?

I have nothing of more importance
    than to tickle my laughing bones

I have done so too - spewing lies
    hoping to be seen as honest

Was I believed or was I someone's show?

I applaud - clapping my hands slow, repeatedly

Smirking my lips while eyebrows squinch
My stomach pains me
My stomach full of comedy

STAGED

I've been the performer
> but
>> I've never seen a show - quite like this

Please, tell me more lies for my personal pleasure
I'll order the bar full of snacks
> and sip a bubbling root beer
> while wishing for
> Dulce De Leche ice cream

Act 98

The ether is serving identities
Choose as you wish

Combine pieces from others'
Choose as you wish

Create your uniqueness
       falling into one
       from the same vibrant closet
       full of collages

Paste your picture
       resembling those already stuck
       minds unalike

The ether is serving identities
Choose until you have exhausted all personality

Choose until you can't define
Choose until you cannot sort

Holding on to identity firmly
But it always slips

Morphing
Molding
Moving

Until you have become them

The eccentric - a stream of main

STAGED

Searching always for fog
Clutter your clothing until you can't see them at all
	becoming one
		woven into complete fabric

Act 99

Careful, they are stealing joy
Stirring up fear like warming stew
Unapologetic - void of guilt
Quietly they watch
Temptation tugs - tearing away barriers
Patience
Time
Determination
They charge in the cold of moon
Studying prey learning their roots of happiness
They harvest the fruits of the farmer

STAGED

I can feel the pain
The residue of my healing
My freedom is to have felt

My prison - dull, dark, numb and damp
My escape - thoughtfully planned

Brimming with anxieties
My courage - bold, big and extroverted

I am the aftermath of my healing
I am now, finally feeling

Act 100

My mind like a train
full of passengers

My thoughts raised the temperature
of my body - burning

My only desire
peace and ease

Flowers and lite rain
kissed the grass on the hill

They have the most peace and ease
they don't shush one another - they just live

My mind
overpacked

My body
isn't pleased

My awareness - heightened

I feel every part of my body

I breathe and become bloated
with the meal of life - unselfishly served

STAGED

to be consumed
in illusions
is to lose sight

temporally fixed
on the dream

we continue to
comfortably sleep

Act 101

I am not a plastic card
I am not digits

Associate with disassociation
Becoming one with ordinary
    all else is Botox

Packaged and wrapped tied with pink bows
    Oh, and it looks appealing
    we better play or else

Lines formless - Our minds imagine them real

Senses experience
    eyes
    mouth
    nose
    skin
    and ears

Fighting with
    hegos
    shegos
    and themgos
    theygos

It's funny - I giggle

STAGED

What we fight for
        must give to those
        who hold innocence
        giving until selfless
        until dust
        until we vanish

Meaning isn't to be found - there is none

We keep watch at clock
        Until our time comes

And when it does
        just maybe you'd be the judge
        of your life lived

Regrettably, or
        fulfilled
        from emptiness

Act 102

Spoonful of hope
Gorgeous medicine

Cure and alleviate
My sickened heart

Send signs of guidance
Light this darkened path

Allow the beauty of the world to be seen

Can I borrow laughter without returning?

What is the lesson that you've given?

I wait in silence
until you speak through it

Act 103

Consumed in angst
Separated from love
Tired and afraid

Uninspired - creations forbidden
Waiting in a steep cave lit only by
      the end of
      melting wax

Time moves like a hippopotamus
Days fleeting while I feel unheard
      because my screams are in the inside
      and echoes resound only within
      so, the silence is a gift to you
      and a burden I *must* bear

If I screamed aloud - infrastructures would collapse
My tragedy spread over your sweet
      bountiful buttered bread

We'd bellow collaboratively - in sync
Creating a symphony with our instruments - voices

I'm selfish with my heartaches

The echoes within bounce off each other

My inner instrumentation
      an enemy of love

Why do I hold on when the echoes cause harm?

STAGED

The wax has melted
Light doesn't touch any walls
My steps make sound
        but not like the echoes
        within

STAGED

104

The remedy rest in vials
I choose the poison - reluctantly
    because I - have wisdom
    and wisdom within knows better
    but I don't listen to the instinctive wisdom

My indecisive rumbling mind
    takes over like clouds
    covering up the ocean sky

The conflict - invisible
Secretive and insidious
Poisoned by the scuffle

    But I am free to choose

The remedy rest in vials
My mind says otherwise
My mind dedicated to suffering
    wired by default

Act 105

Above the clouds

The reality of the world
       fictitious

The happenings

The walks
The screams
The troubles
The smiles

I have been told to drizzle down

Feel into the agony
Feel into the joy
Feel into the anger

To remember
       my heart

Act 106

I haven't awakened
The dream I am dreaming
Feels real
Within it I feel suffocated and numb

Wandering in an abyss of lost
Pungent taste of uncertainty
Life isn't certain

I want to control this dream
The more I try the more
I am endlessly consumed by night

Dreams of living terror
Fear fills until bloated
Waiting for fear's surrender

But fear is bold
Bolder than I

I wish I had fear's courage
The resiliency to be unwavering

Act 107

Love's remnants
Alone and accepted
Clarity emerges
Routines now absent like the heart I once had -
    for them

Finding me
The one I lost years ago
The present me doesn't know much of them

I extended myself to love
Cuddling the exterior
Practicing love

I found the error from my past

My internal giving of love
Lost in extension

Alone - I stand with me
Alone - I have difficult conversation with me
Admitting
Forgiving
And - learning - who I am beneath

I live in creation
Starting from blanks
I am pleased knowing
That freedom exists

STAGED

my
emotion
barricaded
inspiration

Act 108

The lively party and the mourning of a funeral
    lives in my heart

The dancing and the sobbing both came from love

A heart that has no choice but to feel
    the pulsating bass
    the vibration of the screams

The dance moves minding its business
    oozing terrible joy

The funeral aches
    in warming pain

        Within heart

Dancing
Dying
    Busy - with something, always

Tightened
    Opened
Kissed
    Hugged
Throbbed
        Out of love

STAGED

joy is a costume
anger is as well
both are the same
only painted
with a different shade
of color

STAGED

Act 109

Optical illusions
Magic tricks
The command of snapping fingers
        rises the sun

Yawning and stretching
        smelling hints of earth

Another day fills me with
        thankful appreciation of unconditional
        love

Wrapped in protection
The comfort carries on
        without interruption

Trusting
I have learned to trust

Your delicate and mighty hands
        are made to caress

Soothe when I am shaken

Optical illusion

My perceptions made
The portrait against the wall real

        She posed
        without - a smile

How can one be shy
when they live to perform?

STAGED

Act 110

I have been as stiff as a broken tree branch
Stern as a judge declaring life sentence
Laughter, frown upon
I forgot how to
Giggle

I remembered the passings
The lifes - coming back - no more

I remembered my lap
      how I crossed the shore
        and into the ocean from my lap

My physical body remained
But my spirit left like their spirits

I wasn't in good spirits

Grief - like an apocalyptic boom
Targeting my heart

I have been as stiff as a broken tree branch
Stern as a judge declaring life sentence
Laughter, frown upon
I forgot how to
Giggle

I'm remembering joy and presence
I'm remembering the life
      when they were here

The character
is
the
adjective

Act 111

I was visited in my dream last night
I wanted it to last forever

Vivid and expressive

Color to the mundane
Color to the black and white

I haven't seen your picture in a while

I am reminded from these mirrors

The details were perfect

It was like a once upon a time
I know once upon a times aren't real

I watched you through the lens of my mind

It was like a silent movie

You didn't speak

I watched you move as if I wasn't there

I awoke happy to have had you visit
- it didn't feel like a dream

greed is an
expression
of God
an art piece
created to confuse

Act 112

Play because it is medicine
    it keeps one young

Give because
    what you have is unique to you

Share because
    intelligence needs are to duplicate

Fear is poison
    and smothered in regret

Rainbows don't ask for permission
    nor does the tycoons

Time will leave you
    eventually

Your life is not promised

Play before your light flickers

Play before the curtains close

Act 113

Many times
    familiar words slipped

The words that when people hear
    their hearts melt

Their knees
    turn mush

I said it because it was fashionable

All that I am

I never unconditionally
    accepted myself

How could I truly love you
When I have continuously neglected myself?

We bounced around
    in what seemed like love lessons

You taught me to never say those words
    unless I mean them

I taught myself to accept

I taught myself to look within
- and never without

STAGED

I sat under the moon and she whispered

"I have never been much of a mystery
they've sadly forgotten me"

I found love
profound
in darkness

Act 114

My days are a lot different now
I am preoccupied with silence
Your communication vanished
like a mystery of abduction

Funny how moments turn from night to day
I comfort myself now
I am amazed at how life just works out

Disasters create new land - a new beginning

Here I am
I have begun

Guilty no longer
I have nothing to complain for
nothing to hope for

Freedom fell unto my heart
Freedom cleansed my spirit
No longer bound in your fault making

ABOUT THE AUTHOR

Imerald Brown was born in Oakland, CA and raised Nichiren Buddhist. Imerald Brown was considered a "Fortune Baby" meaning that they were born into the Buddhist practice. At a young age Imerald Brown struggled with feelings of embarrassment due to the practices of their mother's faith. Their mother chanted fiercely in the living room facing her Gohonzon while ringing the bell moments after silence. Young Imerald Brown felt anxious and worried about what neighbors and friends would think if they were to hear their mother chanting.

Imerald Brown's mother would have conversations comprising numerous themes of spiritual influence such as death, manifestation, karma, reincarnation, unexplained phenomenon, dreams, and premonitions, etc. In Imerald Brown's fundamental early years these seemingly insightful one-sided dialogues raised fear, doubt and even depression. Imerald Brown felt as though they were the odd family in the neighborhood. Imerald Brown found comfort in music and writing.

As adulthood positioned, Imerald Brown had undoubtably rejoiced in their upbringing as it provided a foundation of their life's journey. Imerald Brown's mother's sentiments began to make sense. Imerald Brown is a lyricist, model, writer, and poet who recently launched an organization to help spread positive messages through Hip Hop, art, life experiences, poetry, and entrepreneurship. Imerald Brown's spirituality is fluid; incorporating different beliefs, faiths and utilizing what resonates while remaining open to learning more.